I believe this book offers another way to describe what God's plan for fallen humanity is through the use of art and the visual presentation. The artist carries beyond literal visual presentation to pictures that conjure deeper thought into the mystery of the cross and God's love for us. This generation is extremely driven and educated through the visual world. It helps them to be drawn into a relationship with God if they can visualize the awe and wonder of the events. The warmth and caring of a loving Father, and His desire to be in right relationship with us for a future filled with hope and meaning. Sometimes art is one of the few things that can tap into things that are subconscious and give the reader a reason to investigate further the claims of Christ.

Greg T. Alexander,
Ekklesia, Toronto Church Planting, Toronto

In Seven Days?

Roslyn Gatts Alexander

CrossBooks™
A Division of LifeWay
1663 Liberty Drive
Bloomington, IN 47403
www.crossbooks.com
Phone: 1-866-879-0502

First published by CrossBooks 6/29/2011

ISBN: 978-1-6150-7884-4 (sc)

Library of Congress Control Number: 2011929977

All digital art and re-storytelling of the Creation story by Roslyn Gatts Alexander © 2008
www.roslynart.com to see Blue Earth

Printed in the United States of America

This book is printed on acid-free paper.

CROSSBOOKS
PUBLISHING

Dedicated to my grandchildren and to the generations of creation's children who will see what He will do!

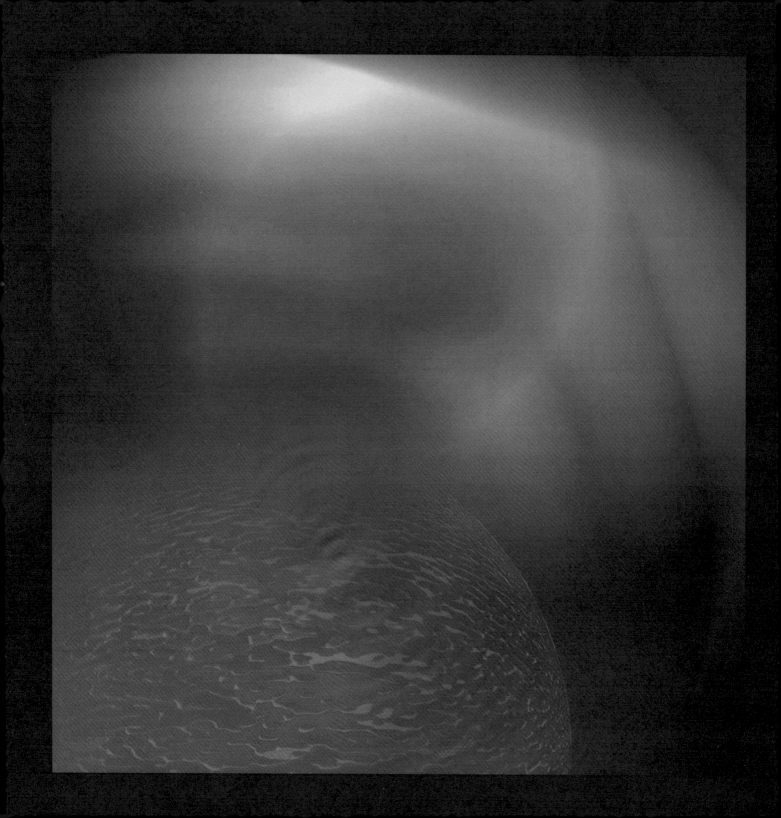

The earth was made in seven days—could this be? A loving God imagined and longed for me? No warm, living creatures looked out into the heavens or swam in the waters deep. No living ear was here to hear a single word God was about to speak.

Genesis 1:1–2
John 1:1–2

On Day One

God spoke, and light came to be so He might experience a day with me. No sun or moon was then seen. Just this energy we now believe is a day that separates light from darkness too, it seems.

Genesis 1:3-5

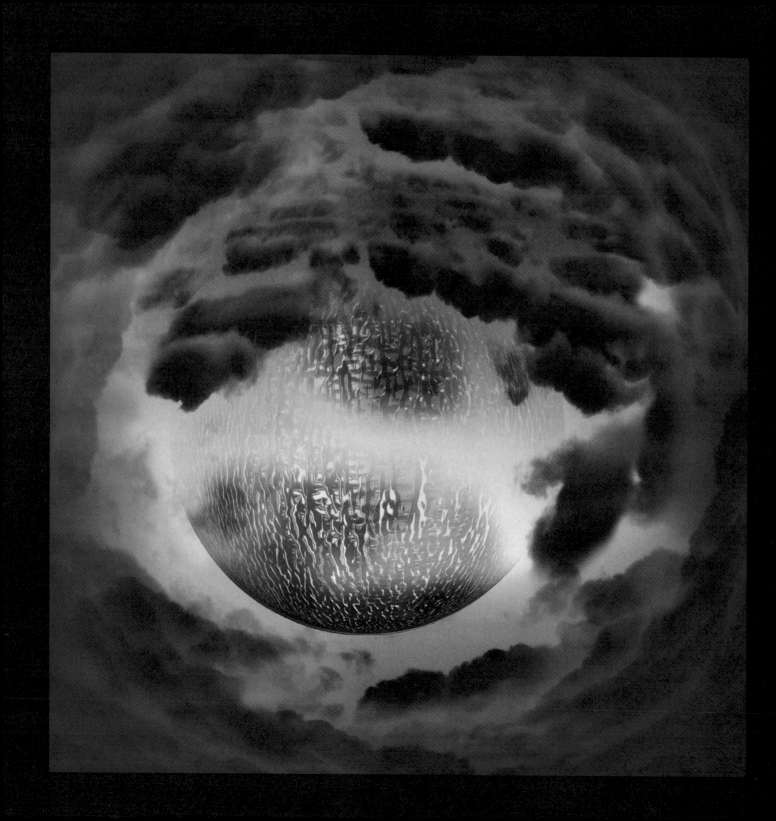

On Day Two

On the second day, the One who sees was still thinking about me as He separated the water, the sky, and the sea.

Genesis 1:3–5

On Day Three

God thought about the food I would need the colors I would see, the smells, the tastes, and the views— all that He already knew. God planned this all before it was so. He planned all this so I would know—from the tiniest seed to the grandest tree, I could see and understand who made me!

Genesis 1:9–13

On Day Four

God brought forth the beauty of His heavenly home. One sun to light up the day, and one moon to reflect the sun's energy, so in darkness, we might see.

Wait! If this is day four, then what came before? Three days without sunlight—yet somehow life was already taking form?

Yes, that's how His Word reads—but that is not all. Planets aligned with gravitational pull; all this was done so we would know that the God of the universe is in control.
God is timeless and existed unthinkably long before day four. A curtain of stars hangs over our earthly home so we might understand our Father's glory and love—but there is more …

Genesis 1:14–19

On Day Five

The ocean's roar was heard on high. Life plunged into the oceans deep and sailed up high. Winged creatures sang their praises from the tops of trees into the winds or through the deepest seas—each was designed just as it should be.

Genesis 1:20–24

14

On Day Six

God spoke, and all living creatures awoke. Land-roaming beasts and mountain goats climbed high on peaks. Creatures of every kind sprang up from their hinds, leaping up to the sound of the creator's call:

"Let there be."

On day six, God looked and saw—but that was not all. He thought of me and created Adam and Eve.

God saw that all life was good. All creation lifted up their sounds, calling, "Abba, Father, Creator" out loud. From the tops of mountains to the deepest of seas, all creation was one with the creator—all that there was and ever will be.

Genesis 1:26–27, Psalm 8:4

16

On Day Seven

God everlasting was here to stay with mankind on the seventh day. Our creation complete, the planets aligned, the heavens aglow as God rested and made this day holy as He separated it for rest.

One day each week, we stop, restore, and remember our Maker, who formed us for fellowship with Him.

Sunday!

Lord, help us all to better understand Your love for us!

Genesis 2:1–3

Day of Sin

The crafty serpent came to Eve with a lie and a plan to cause her to sin.
When Adam did not protest, darkness and fear came here to stay.
God slew an animal for its skin and showed them how to sew clothes for
this cold life of sin. He sent them to work for their food with thistles and
thorns; the earth was affected by their sin too, I suppose.

They both longed to be back in the garden with their lives restored.
Darkness and pain came into the world on that horrible day when Adam
and Eve looked away from the creator of day.

God sent an angel to drive them away from their paradise home so their
hearts might return to their creator once more.

God knew a way to redeem men and women from their sin. Jesus Christ,
God's only Son, was with Him from the beginning too, it appears.

Genesis 1:26, Genesis 3:2, Isaiah 9:2, John 1:10

This New Day

In seven days, not measured by our limited view of sun and moon, God provided life to all living things we know. On this new day of grace, God offers eternal life to humankind again.

In a timeless paradise called heaven, He offers us a new life with Him! God did this by sending His Son to live and then die for our sins on the cross.
Christ took my place and stepped in between, preventing my eternal punishment for sin.

Will you ask Christ to come live deep within?

God will understand your desire to make things right with Him. Jesus will make us whole with the creator again.

Psalm 22:25–26, Isaiah 53:11

A Day with God as our Light

God spoke light into this cold, dark sphere and gave us His word so we might know Him. He gave us His Son to show us His love and offers us new life when we invite Christ to come. God almighty has not turned us away, but sustains us in trials if we believe in Him this day. No one can imagine what else God has prepared for those who love Him and seek Him today—and there is more ...

"The sun will no more be your light by day nor will the brightness of the moon shine on you, for the LORD will be your everlasting light and your God will be your glory" (Isaiah 60:19, NIV).

1 Corinthians 2:9, 2 Peter 1:19, Luke 21:33

About the Author

Roslyn was born in Columbus Ohio, as the middle child of five children.

She holds a Board of Governor degree with a minor in fine art from Eastern Illinois University. She also has an Applied Science degree in Occupational Therapy from Parkland College, Champaign, Illinois. Over the past seventeen years Roslyn has worked with children and adults with special needs teaching and equipping her clients with skills for everyday living, fine motor skills for handwriting and arts and crafts.

Roslyn and her husband Greg are now church planting in the Greater Toronto Area of Canada where Roslyn continues to assist children with developmental delays.

Roslyn has been involved in the local church and collegiate ministry along side her husband of 36 years. Greg and Roslyn raised two children and have three grandchildren that have been an inspiration for her books.

Roslyn also studied art at Kansas University, Lawrence, Kansas and Montgomery College, Rockville, Maryland.

Roslyn stated that in 1974 her father Robert Roswell Gatts, Dean of Mechanical Engineering at Kansas University, told her that some day she would be able to make art on the computer.

After taking a Photoshop workshop in 2001 at the University of Illinois, Springfield she started creating digital art. In the years 2002-2005 Roslyn showed and sold her work at a variety of venues in Springfield, Illinois.

In 2008 she composed the books In Seven Days?, and Blue Earth, with some of her first digital art pieces. Blue Earth is now a digital track anyone can view on line or download at http://www.roslynart.com/roslynart/Blue_Earth_pp.html

Roslyn has also published Bread of Presence, Jesus has always been with us, and she has two more books on the drawing board.

CPSIA information can be obtained
at www.ICGtesting.com
Printed in the USA
250327LV00001B